AT RISK

BOMB SQUADS &
SWAT TEAMS

BY
Jean Dick

EDITED BY
Anita Larsen

PUBLISHED BY
CRESTWOOD HOUSE
Mankato, MN, U.S.A.

CIP

LIBRARY OF CONGRESS CATALOGING IN PUBLICATION DATA

Dick, Jean.
　Bomb squads and SWAT teams.

　(At risk)
　Includes index.
　SUMMARY: Describes the history, activities, equipment, and special
training of SWAT teams and bomb squads.
　　1. Police—United States—special weapons and tactics units—Juvenile
literature. 2. Bombing investigation—United States—Juvenile literature.
[1. Police—Special weapons and tactics units. 2. Bombing investigation.
3. Occupations.] I. Larsen, Anita. II. Title. III. Title: Bomb squads and SWAT
teams. IV. Series.
HV8080.S64D54　1988　　　　　363.2'32—dc19　　　　　88-15907
ISBN 0-89686-401-4

International Standard
Book Number:
0-89686-401-4

Library of Congress
Catalog Card Number:
88-15907

PHOTO CREDITS

Cover: Wide World Photos: David Bookstaver
Gloria Blockey: 4, 33
Rosemary Grimm: 8-9, 19, 23, 25, 26-27, 28-29, 30, 35, 39
Journalism Services: (John Patsch) 10, 13, 17
DRK Photo: (Don & Pat Valenti) 37
Wide World Photos: 34; (Mario Suriani) 7; (David Bookstaver) 14;
(David Longstreath) 20-21, 42

Produced by Carnival Enterprises.

CRESTWOOD HOUSE

Box 3427, Mankato, MN, U.S.A. 56002

TABLE OF CONTENTS

A DANGEROUS OCCUPATION

In New York City, two members of a special police unit, a SWAT team, answered an early morning call. A man was threatening to jump from a 12-inch ledge on the World Trade Center, high above the city.

The SWAT team officers who answered the call went to work immediately. The officers talked quietly and steadily to the jumper. They convinced him to get off the ledge. Their job was well done, and it was a great thrill for them to have saved a life. This was why they had joined the SWAT team.

On Saturday, February 8, 1986, Los Angeles Police Department bomb squad officers Arleigh McCree and Ronald Ball were called to a home. Two pipe bombs had been found there. With over 38 years of police experience between them, this wasn't their first call. But it turned out to be their last.

Officers McCree and Ball were killed instantly when the bombs they were trying to defuse exploded. "It could happen to anyone," said one of their fellow officers. "McCree was the best in the world."

Binoculars, flashlights, weapons, and ammunition are part of a SWAT team member's gear.

ALWAYS ON THE JOB

All police work is a way of life, not just a job. Officers must be ready to protect us 24 hours a day. They control traffic to get students to school safely. Our neighborhoods are safer because of them. They arrest criminals and appear in court to be sure that the guilty go to jail. They help settle day-to-day conflicts, too.

Emergencies call for special teams, like bomb squads and SWAT teams. Hostages in an airplane hijacking or office workers threatened by a bomb hidden in a public building know that police officers risk their own lives to save others.

"A SUSPICIOUS PACKAGE"

Sergeant Jordan of the 85th Precinct's bomb squad had just finished his paperwork and was sitting down for a cup of coffee when the telephone rang.

"I'm calling from a gas station near County Road 45 and Highway 1," the voice over the phone said. "There's a suspicious package in the field where I've been working. It's ticking. Can you come right away?"

A bomb squad member's equipment includes a helmet and a thickly-padded suit.

"I'll be right there," said Jordan. He remembered that a new powerline was being built in that area. There had been protests and threats. This could be the real thing. In fact, a threat is always treated as the real thing until proven otherwise.

Sergeant Jordan called his partner, Officer Phillips. They met at the bomb truck and in minutes the bomb squad was in motion. At the same time police squad cars rushed to the scene and evacuated the area.

When Officers Jordan and Phillips arrived, the area was clear. They parked their truck a safe distance away and put on the 49-pound bomb suits that shield their bodies. Now they were ready to

A bomb squad trailer is built to carry unexploded bombs away from people to a place where the bomb can be set off safely.

move in for a closer look at the package. They heard steady ticking coming from the package and moved quickly back to the truck.

"Should we jar it?" Phillips asked. The officers

can tell if a package will explode at a touch by using a remote control device.

"How about moving it with the bomb trailer?" suggested Jordan.

9

When no one is in danger, the bomb squad may decide to set off a bomb with the help of a remote control device.

"No, the area is clear, and no one will be hurt if the bomb goes off right now. We don't need to move it."

"Maybe we should defuse it with a water cannon." This stream of water under high pressure can separate the power source from the blasting cap.

"Let's detonate," decided Phillips. "The area is clear. There's no danger to anything or anybody."

Jordan agreed. The bomb squad uses remote control to set off bombs. They prepared their equipment and called out the warning:

"Fire in the hole! Fire in the hole! Fire in the hole!"

They then fired the "hell box" and a huge explosion filled the air. The sky turned grey with dirt and the ground shook. The officers made the right decision. The bomb was real. It was safely detonated, and no one was hurt. When a bomb is defused in this way, it is called a "high order detonation."

The bomb squad drove back to headquarters to write a report.

WHO ARE THE BOMB SQUAD OFFICERS?

Special teams work, which involves inspecting "suspicious packages," is risky—and it's not for everyone. Split-second decisions can mean life or death for both the officers and bystanders. Long hours filled with threat of injuries or death are all in a day's work. So are the thrills and rewards that come from saving lives.

Police officers volunteer for jobs on the bomb squad. They must have at least three years of experience in law enforcement work. They attend special classes in addition to regular training. This training emphasizes safety and helps reduce the risks of the job.

Bomb squad officers are always cautious, knowing that what they're handling can kill them. Every suspicious package is treated with respect. Rows of plaques on the squad room walls honor those who have died in the line of duty. They are constant reminders of the dangers these officers face every day.

BOMB SQUAD TRAINING

In a high-risk job, training may mean the difference between life and death. Each member on a bomb squad is carefully and thoroughly trained.

New bomb squad recruits are sent to Hazardous Device School for four weeks of training. This school is run by the Federal Bureau of Investigation (FBI) and the U.S. Army in Huntsville, Alabama. Before

A bomb can come in many different shapes—and a bomb squad member must be suspicious of every shape.

13

Bomb squad members must work quickly to evacuate a building where a bomb has been reported.

recruits are accepted, their departments must agree to buy nearly $100,000 worth of safety equipment. The typical list of equipment includes bomb suits, bomb blankets, X-ray machines, listening devices, metal detectors, self-contained breathing equipment, and special vehicles for transporting live bombs. Robots and trained dogs round out the list for most bomb squads.

The training in Alabama begins in the classroom where recruits learn to identify bombs. The classroom is full of bombs that experienced officers have defused. A foot-long pipe cut in half shows how a pipe-bomb was constructed. Little pipe bombs only two or three inches long are also studied. An innocent-looking book opens to reveal explosives and a timing device that could kill when the bomb explodes. Cigar boxes or children's school boxes are used that way, too.

Of course not every bomb is disguised. Recruits study hand grenades, blasting caps, and dynamite. Safety is always emphasized.

"Hoax bombs" are also studied. These are bright red sticks of pretend-dynamite held together with a timer. They're sold in novelty stores. "Some people think that these are funny," said one officer. "We don't." The officer added that real bombs are almost never as obvious as this.

M-80's, large and legal fireworks sold for the 4th of July, are another kind of explosive studied. Much larger, and illegal versions are used by terrorists. Bomb squad officers cautioned that even M-80's can blow off an arm or leg or even kill someone.

Finally, officers learn to look out for booby traps. Doors and drawers can be wired to blow up when they're opened. There is no limit to the ways that terrorists can make bombs. Through training, bomb squad officers hope to limit their risks.

Bomb squad recruits continue their training by learning to defuse and dismantle bombs. A course in investigation teaches them to study whatever is left after a bomb goes off. They examine the materials and try to trace them back to the person who bought them. They also look at the construction and design to see if they can recognize the style of a known terrorist.

Yearly refresher courses help bomb squad officers keep a step ahead of terrorists. They often spend a week learning about the latest technology. This could be anything from new robots to air-conditioned bomb suits.

Weekly, less formal training, is provided by the bomb squad departments themselves. Officers practice putting on bomb suits and gas masks or using their robots. They study the latest bomb they've found or discuss articles they've read about new technology.

HOW THE BOMB SQUAD WORKS

When a bomb squad call comes in from the police department, at least two officers are sent. They drive to the scene in a bomb truck that carries all of their special equipment. "The drive is the hardest part,"

Bombs are dangerous and can flare up suddenly.

said one officer. "When we get there we turn off everything else in our heads and focus on one thing—the bomb."

They frequently use X-ray equipment to find out if the suspicious package is deadly or harmless. Many times, packages are only made up to look like bombs. This, too, is a serious crime.

The location of the package determines how it will be handled. If it's in an open area where no one could get hurt, it is sometimes jarred and then set off with an explosive charge.

When it's in an area where there could be danger to people or property, it may need to be moved to a safer place in a bomb trailer. Such trailers are heavily fortified and weigh over four tons. They are designed to contain the explosion and explode, or "vent," it safely up into the air.

Few bombs are defused by humans these days. Dogs are trained to sniff out explosives, and robots do the dangerous work of defusing bombs. "If the worst happens and a bomb explodes," said one police sergeant, "you've only lost equipment, not a human life."

Most police dogs are German Shepherds, but Doberman Pinschers and Rottweilers are also used. They are trained constantly. The dogs live in the police officer's home and become trusted family pets. As part of their training, police dogs learn not to jar any package that they've found. Moving a bomb just a little might be enough to set it off.

Robots are now commonly used to dismantle bombs. They are directed by remote control by the officers safely in their bomb truck. Using robots to defuse bombs was an idea brought to the United States by the British. Robots are used routinely in Northern Ireland, where bombings are a frequent threat.

If the robot successfully defuses a bomb, the officers use the pieces as evidence to track down the person who made the bomb. They may find several sticks of dynamite, a blasting cap, a nine-volt battery, and a pocket watch or clock. Whatever is found can give clues to who made it.

Bomb squad officers never take anything for granted. The size of a package means nothing. A small, innocent-looking box can blow up a building, killing everyone in and around it. One officer said, "The fear of failure is the secret of success. If you're not sweating when you've finished a job, you're doing something wrong."

Robots have long arms and metal fingers to grasp a bomb and dismantle it.

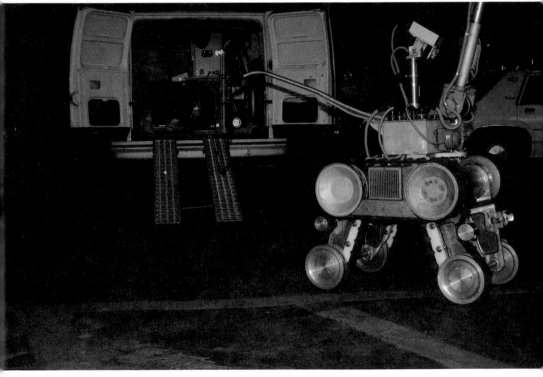

Members of a SWAT team are always cautious.

SWAT TEAMS

SWAT stands for Special Weapons And Tactics Team or Special Weapons Attack Team. Some police departments use different names like CIRT (Critical Incident Response Team) or ESU (Emergency Services Unit).

Whatever their name, their mission is the same. They're the special police department units that rescue hostages, stop snipers, or prevent assassinations. They're called in to talk down a jumper, capture terrorists, or protect visiting dignitaries. The safety of people at special events like the Olympic Games depends on the SWAT team.

They protect people when problems are expected or threatened. For example, when the 1986 centennial celebration of the Statue of Liberty was held in New York City, more than 20,000 police officers were on duty to protect millions of visitors. Many of these officers were members of SWAT teams or bomb squads. Seven robots, ten explosive-sniffing dogs, and four bomb trucks stood ready to help them.

TERRORISM

One of the most important jobs of a SWAT team is to deal with terrorists. Terrorists are people who threaten lives and property for political reasons. In 1977, there were 112 terrorist incidents in the United States. Airplanes were hijacked and passengers and crews were taken hostage. Innocent people were killed by snipers.

In June 1985, TWA Flight 847 was hijacked on a flight from Athens to Rome. There were 153 passengers and a crew aboard the flight. Two Shi'ite Muslims took control. "He has pulled a hand-grenade pin and is ready to blow up the aircraft if he

SWAT teams enter buildings carefully and in groups—they never know what they'll find inside.

has to," said the pilot. Passengers were beaten, and one was killed before this dramatic hijacking ended.

Ships are threatened, too. In October 1985, the ship *Achille Lauro* was hijacked, and a passenger in a wheelchair was killed.

State and local authorities work together with the FBI to fight terrorism. Many cities have formed joint task forces. In most large cities, the FBI has a local office. SWAT teams from all levels are ready to act immediately when a terrorist act is committed. "Combating terrorism is a job for all law enforcement agencies," said one SWAT team officer. "It's a major problem, but we're happy to report that the number of threats has been reduced since 1977."

WHO ARE THE SWAT TEAM OFFICERS?

Like bomb squad officers, SWAT team members are experienced police officers who volunteer for this special team. SWAT teams look for team players. Everyone's survival depends on it. It's so important that SWAT teams often vote on whether a volunteer can join their team.

Maturity, discipline, and emotional strength are very important characteristics for SWAT team officers. Before volunteers are accepted, they must

SWAT team members must be able to work together to catch a terrorist or stop a sniper.

A SWAT team's "shooters" are excellent marksmen.

pass interviews and tests. They must also agree to attend ongoing training.

SWAT team members develop a tremendous amount of trust in one another. It's essential. Having that attitude helps officers carry out orders immediately.

SWAT TEAM
SPECIALTIES

SWAT teams are often divided into three groups. "Shooters" are expert marksmen who can hit a target

Sometimes "talkers" must use a mike and speaker to communicate with criminals inside a building.

from a long distance. They are called in when snipers or hostage takers have gained control of an area and are threatening the lives of innocent people.

"Talkers" have good communication skills. They try to talk down a person who wants to jump off a

building. They also try to get hostage takers to release their captives. These officers are chosen because they listen and communicate well. They can develop trust quickly with a person they often can't even see.

The third SWAT team group is the "entry team." This group, usually made up of four or five officers, breaks down doors to surprise and arrest suspects. "These officers are the gutsiest group," one officer said. "There's always a good chance that they'll meet a gun on the other side of the door."

Entry teams are now commonly used to enter well-fortified houses where drugs are used and sold. First they get a "no knock" search warrant from a

When other methods fail to disarm criminals inside a building, the "entry team" is called in.

judge. This makes it legal to enter a suspect's house without permission. Then they ram down the door before the suspects can flush the drugs or other evidence down the toilet.

Early in 1984, the Los Angeles Police Department used something new to ram down doors—an eight-ton tank-like vehicle equipped with a battering ram. The vehicle caused a lot of controversy. "That tank belongs on a battlefield, not in a neighborhood," was a common complaint. Others said criminals can turn a neighborhood into a war zone. The tank is still used by officers who have a court order.

In Minnesota in January 1988, a front-end loader crashed through the wall of a suspected illegal drug-making location. Special entry team officers were close behind the loader to arrest the suspect. Speed is as important as surprise in a successful operation so that no one gets hurt.

These new techniques were developed because drug dealers have started fortifying their homes with bars and steel doors. Ordinary battering rams don't do the job anymore. Police sometimes call these homes "rock houses," because they are built so solidly.

Recently a new technique has been tried—explosive entry. Camouflaged SWAT team officers place an explosive wire around the door. A safe distance away, they set off the explosive, which acts like a cutting torch. An archway is made quickly and without much damage inside. "It's fast and it's safe," said one officer. "People standing only ten feet away aren't even hurt. They're sure surprised, though."

SPECIAL TRAINING

SWAT team recruits get specialized training that builds on what they've already learned. They get extensive emergency medical training that makes them almost like emergency medical technicians. They learn how to remove injured people safely from an accident and how to stop bleeding. They can also help a heart attack victim using cardiopulmonary resuscitation (CPR).

Special weapons training emphasizes accuracy from long distances. Recruits spend hours on the practice range shooting at targets hundreds of yards away.

Communications training helps the SWAT team talk to and listen to people who are threatening others. A jumper's life can be saved by an officer if he can "talk" him back inside a building. "Words are our weapons," said one officer. It is their job to reason with a suspect before resorting to force.

Learning how to handle tear gas is another specialty. "Ten minutes with a gas mask on is a long time," one officer exclaimed. "It's tight. It's hot. It's hard to breath, and it's hard to see when it fogs up."

SWAT team members need to aim accurately when they shoot tear gas.

During training, SWAT team members sharpen their skills.

Tear gas specialists learn how to throw or fire tear gas accurately, then work quickly to make arrests or rescues.

Some SWAT teams even learn how to rappel, or climb down sheer cliffs or buildings. Sometimes that's how they rescue people or find weapons or evidence.

A SWAT TEAM TRAINING DRILL

SWAT teams use training exercises to help them learn. In one exercise, a sergeant describes an

A heavy, protective plate shields the SWAT team member from gun fire.

imaginary hostage situation in great detail. A team of officers decides what to do, beginning with the call to the police.

They ask questions to help them decide on action: Is the threat real? Can we talk to the terrorist? How many hostages are there? Is there a demand for ransom money? Where can we get the money?

The SWAT team also discusses coordination with telephone, gas, and utility companies. A simple step such as cutting off electricity may intimidate the suspect into giving up. If the terrorist demands an airplane, SWAT members work with the airport, the fire department, and a nearby hospital.

They also consider what to wear. Will their 20-

pound body armor be enough protection, or do they need another ten pounds of special plates? These drills help SWAT teams prepare for the risks they face every day.

EARLY LAW ENFORCEMENT

Throughout history, ideas have changed about how a police force—and how a bomb squad and SWAT team—treats criminals.

The early colonists who settled in America thought police power should be limited. That idea is written into our Constitution and Bill of Rights. The Fourth Amendment says that there should be no "unreasonable" searches and seizures (arrests).

In the late 1860s, the Fourteenth Amendment was ratified. The Constitution's restrictions were extended to each state. Because of this amendment, SWAT teams must go to a judge and ask for a court order before they break into private property.

Americans believe in local control of police departments. The more than 20,000 different law enforcement agencies in America are all independent. Small towns, county sheriffs, and large city police departments divide duties. They cooperate when they need special help, just as the FBI and local police work together to fight terrorism. In Connecticut, for example, a state trooper developed a lead that led to the arrest of a man who had been on the FBI's Ten Most Wanted List for many years.

Early in the 1900s, both the FBI and state police were created. Between 1920 and 1960, revolutionary changes were made in United States police departments. Some changes came from technology: patrol cars, two-way radios, and telephones are examples. Other changes came because police

Bomb squads and SWAT teams work closely with city police.

officers were better trained and departments hired more full-time officers.

A police crisis developed in the 1960s. The civil rights movement and protests against American involvement in the Vietnam War caused unrest across the country. Riots broke out in many cities. Police often used harsh methods to stop them.

It was a time of many changes. There were new risks, too. Police and SWAT teams called to break up anti-war demonstrations were sometimes pelted with rocks and bottles. College students, not criminals, were fighting back.

TODAY'S POLICE FORCE

Today, bomb squad and SWAT team members have to be police officers. They must meet the usual police department requirements. One of these is a high school education. More and more police departments are encouraging recruits to have some college training in law enforcement, too.

Many junior colleges, colleges, and universities offer programs in law enforcement or administration of justice. Course work includes instruction in the law, civil rights, state and local ordinances, use of

A SWAT team receives the next assignment.

firearms, self-defense, first aid, and accident investigation. Police academies also offer training.

Physical education and sports are especially helpful in developing the stamina and agility needed for police work. Knowing a foreign language helps, too. In some neighborhoods in Houston, Texas, for example, Spanish is more common than English.

The kinds of training recruits receive before their first assignment are varied. In small towns, training could mean going along with an experienced officer for a few days. In larger cities, it could mean 50 hours in the classroom and six to seven weeks of on-the-job training. The one thing that remains the same is that a bomb squad or SWAT team member's education never really ends.

In addition to education requirements, police officers must also meet civil service requirements. These are government rules that apply to nearly all police officers. Generally, candidates must be U.S. citizens who are at least 21 years old but under 34 years old when they first apply. They have to pass a written test and a physical examination that measures vision, strength, and agility.

Every applicant is investigated. This is to avoid hiring someone with a criminal history. Public records are checked. Friends and past employers are interviewed, too.

Some candidates are also interviewed by a psychiatrist. This helps to discover people with mental illnesses or behavior that does not meet police department standards.

Finally, about half of all police departments require that officers live in the city they work in. They want their officers to be close to the job. Other departments have a requirement that officers live within 35 minutes of their station.

If this sounds like a rigorous set of tests, it is. Police officers and bomb squad and SWAT team members need to be highly trained to meet the risks of today's changing world. Terrorism, drug dealing, and even technology, have made fighting crime a very tough business.

The police department's tests change as rapidly as the risks do. Remember, one of the risks police face is meeting changing ideas of the people they serve.

In the past, for example, minimum height and weight requirements were common. They have been challenged in court by women and minorities who say that these minimums discriminate against them. "Just because I'm not five feet nine inches tall doesn't mean that I won't be a good police officer," one woman said. Many departments have now changed their requirements so that more women and minorities will qualify.

The majority of police officers in the United States today are white males. "Affirmative action" laws are being used to try to recruit more women and minorities.

Surveys show these laws are being followed. In 1982, police departments nationwide had 3.2% women and 7.6% minorities. By 1986, these figures had changed. There were 7.6% women and 18.9% minorities.

Bomb squad and SWAT team members are on call 24 hours a day.

RISING TO THE RISKS

In recent years, a bomb squad or SWAT team officer's duties have revealed unexpected risks. One is that the public sometimes doesn't believe police do enough for them. This adds stress to police work. Police officers try to reduce some of the stress by improving their image with the public. "We've developed programs to teach people how to fight crime," said one community service officer.

Another stress in bomb squad or SWAT team work is being on call 24 hours a day. Most police officers work 40 hours a week, but they can be called any time for emergencies.

In large cities, police officers are specialized. In addition to bomb squads and SWAT teams, you might find motorcycle police, harbor or border patrols, helicopter patrols, canine corps, or youth aid services.

There is another fact that can lead to stress. A police officer can be a hero or a villain in the same day. A dramatic rescue of a small child from a cliff brings both personal rewards and praise from the public. But using tear gas on citizens protesting in public brings catcalls and angry protests.

The stress of police work hits officers' families, too. The threat of danger is always present. The divorce rate among police officers is one of the highest of all occupations.

There is stress, too, from the hours of paperwork and red tape that are part of the job. "It's terribly discouraging," said one officer, "to see a criminal set free by the courts because some paperwork or procedure was not followed."

Another officer expressed his frustration: "We have to answer to everyone—to the public, the captain, and to each other. It's not easy to be right all the time. In this job if you're not right, you might be dead."

The dangers of the job itself are obvious. The effects of stress are hidden. Sleeplessness, ulcers, and high blood pressure are just a few problems that can be brought on by stress. In an effort to fight these problems, or even prevent them, police departments offer help. Physical fitness programs and counseling are made available to all officers.

WHY DO THIS WORK?

Police work is difficult enough. Defusing bombs and dealing with terrorists is even riskier. What makes people do this? Why do they volunteer?

"I like it," said one officer. He, like many of his fellow officers, enjoys helping the public in a very special way. When they come home at night after freeing ten people from a supermarket holdup, they know they've done something important.

Along with the risks, police officers find rewards. Special teamwork helps them learn new skills and make more money. Los Angeles bomb squad officers earn 17% more than patrolmen, for example.

Jobs are secure and layoffs rare. They can retire early, too, often with half-pay after 20 years of service. "I retired at age 50," said one officer, "and started a second career."

In the late 1980s, the salary for beginning police officers was nearly $20,000. With training provided by the department, an officer can move up to sergeant, lieutenant, or captain.

Most large cities have bomb squads with at least one full-time officer and several part-time officers. The same is true for SWAT teams.

Bomb squad and SWAT team members share a lot. They share risks and joys, highs and lows. They have job security, but no guarantee that they'll live to retirement. They're praised and criticized by the public they serve. It's not a job for everyone. But it's wonderful work for those who love it!

FOR MORE INFORMATION

For more information about bomb squads or SWAT teams, write to:

Federal Bureau of Investigation
Washington, D.C., 20535

GLOSSARY/INDEX

GLOSSARY/INDEX

includes expert marksmen. Even from a long distance, shooters can accurately hit a target.

Talkers 28—A group of SWAT team members who talk to and reason with a suspect before using force. For example, talkers will encourage a jumper to get off a ledge.

Tear gas 32, 34, 43—A gas that blinds a person temporarily. It is used to break up crowds or force someone out of a building.

Terrorism 22, 24, 37, 41—The unlawful use of force or violence to intimidate or coerce a government or civilians to change political or social policies.

Water cannon 11—A device used to defuse a bomb using a high pressure stream of water to separate the blasting cap from the power source.

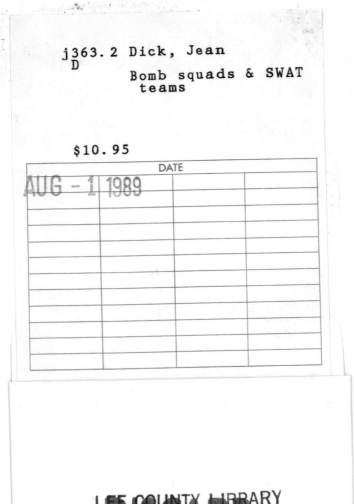

j363.2 Dick, Jean
D
      Bomb squads & SWAT
      teams

$10.95

DATE		
AUG - 1 1989		

© THE BAKER & TAYLOR CO.